Thoughts From The Stour Banks

Glenn Collins

BookLeaf Publishing

Presentation by *BookLeaf Publishing*

Web: www.bookleafpub.com

E-mail: info@bookleafpub.com

ISBN: 9789357213158

First edition 2023

Workplace Friends

Workplace friends are a saving grace,
A grain of calm in a mutinous place.
Colleagues they forever come and go,
But when a friendship bonds you just know.
And when the time comes to bid goodbye,
You wish them well and do not cry.
Something I pondered with this last line,
Where would I be without these friends of mine.

Time

The Time has come for lowered guards,
Check the stakes and play the cards.
Scared or brave, make the call,
Play it safe? Or, go for all?
Time doesn't wait, I've come to see.
After all the past took from me.
So a question asked, for the answer I'll wait...
Is it time that holds our fate?

How've You Been?

Come walk with me,
Through a workplace scene.
19 months...
Tell me, How've you been?

Masks and sanitiser
A reminder of what we went through
Distanced desks,
Old office but this is new.

Glance left and right
Catch a smile, share some memes.
We're back to our normal,
Sharing the love between friends and teams

# #

Hashtags, follow backs,
Watching movies on a mobile phone.
Over 2000 followers but,
You've never felt more alone.

Complain about a life,
But advertise it on the 'gram
In love, fuming, ooh drama!
OMG - DM me fam?!

So it seems to me,
We traded reality,
For connectivity
Trading social for socials
Preferring to Snapchat
Than meet to chat.
"A quick game on the PC?"
Rather than debate PC over coffee

The Beautiful Game

"It's our year" is the dream,
Of every fan, of every team.
It is The Beautiful Game,
Football is it's name.

A pie and A pint,
The pre-match ritual.
The singing of the crowd,
The togetherness is spiritual.

When it comes down to the nitty gritty,
It doesn't matter if your Arsenal or Spurs
or even Man. City.
Because we all feel the same,
The moment our striker takes aim,
We're fans, United, by the beautiful game

Perfect Contrast

The Clutch drops,
Engine Pops,
The Adrenaline rush is surreal.

It's perfectly contrast
A bike moving so fast
But time seems to remain still

Lockdown Thoughts

Objectivising depression as motivation,
Beautifying friendships for appreciation.
Revisiting loneliness and desperation,
Incomprehensibility of adaptation.
However, a revolution in confidence,
Accelerated the differences,
Of harmonious, self satisfaction.

The Forbidden Tree

On the outskirts of the town,
Along the lane you mustn't go down.
Stands the old Forbidden Tree,
Dark and enchanting as can be.

A presence, menacing and foreboding,
It whistles and rustles in the wind.
It inches ever closer, now almost goading,
As if to lure you in.

"I am The Forbidden Tree,
And in these fields I stand,
A warning to all Enmity,
As a defender, of this land."

Last Summer

We didn't know it was your last summer,
Until the joy turned to despair.
Then the smiles turned to tears,
Gazing upon your empty chair.
Physically you're not here,
But I know your always there,
Your laughter fills the hallway,
Your scent lingers in the air

Storm

Batten down the hatches,
Lock up all the doors,
There's a storm front coming,
Like no other before.

As the waves come crashing,
And the rain starts lashing,
The torrent is gathering power,
So, sit tight, and wait each passing hour.

Because when the storm has passed,
And the calm is here at last,
Remember this lifelong truth...
You must endure the rough,
To appreciate the smooth

Want Away

My mind is burning, with these thoughts inside,
All I'm learning is there's nowhere to hide.
Can I roll away like an ocean tide?
Start again on the other side.

All You Do

Whilst there may be doubts in everyone,
Keep on going until you've done.
If you keep the strength to pull through
It will shine in all you do

13 - Unlucky for some

So, how can it be,
That 13 is unlucky?
It's just a number,
Written with a 1 and 3.

But a look through history,
Tells tales of tragedy,
Memories of misery,
all connected to 13.

And if the 13th should be Friday,
Take extra care or even hide away.
Because a menace awaits, upon that date,
And it may just seal your fate.

The Gardens of Home

Recalling memories of my childhood,
The endless fields and Poulders Park.
The friendships of the neighbourhood,
Kicking footballs after dark,

These are more than happy memories,
It's a heart forged in Kentish stone.
Whenever I smell Lavender and Berries,
It reminds me of my home.

Writer's Block

Tap the pen on the table,
Scroll through apps on the phone.
Search for something inspirational,
To find the words you can hone.

Pick a word at random,
Think up a clever rhyme,
Whatever rhymes with tandem?
Oh well better luck next time.

Come back three days later,
And you're up against the clock.
The desperation's now greater,
But you still have writer's block

City Lights

Against the back drop of sunset,
The shimmering streetlight,
Create such beautiful contrast,
A picture perfect, artist's delight.

The reflections in the river,
A beauty that makes me quiver.
The wonders, of this fair city,
Illuminated and oh so pretty.

More Tea?

It's more than just a drink,
It's an opportunity to think.
A catch up with old friends,
Or build bridges and make amends

The first brew of the day,
Hit's the spot and sits just right,
Whether it's PG Tips or an Earl Grey.
Get's you ready for a daily plight.

When I wake up, Or just before sleep,
Coco or Coffee you can keep.
No matter where I'll be,
I'll answer affirmatively when asked...

More Tea?

Everything's Changing

With a click of a button,
We can find out anything that's known,
Do the shopping, pay our bills,
Without leaving home.

Everything's changing,
From what we use to know,
Those days are not returning,
We've only got one way to go.

Anxiety

The cold sweats in the middle of night,
Shaking and trembling nothing feels right.
Trying to breathe as my chest gets tight,
Every sense saying I'm doomed to my plight.

I can get through this, I'm sure.
I've done it a hundred times before.
Feel my heart pounding through my chest,
This anxiety won't kill me, but it's doing it's best.

When it ends and possible causes are mused,
There's no trace on the body,
It's not battered or bruised.
It's all in the mind, be it overused,
Or just misused and abused.

Christmas in Sandwich

Crisp winters days and frosty nights.
Smell of chimneys and those festive lights,
The countdown has begun.
Hug loved ones and see old friends,
Drinks with colleagues, fun never ends.

Times have changed over the years,
For missing loved one's we shed tears.
Toast their names with a glass of wine,
And that delicious feast, on which we dine.
All these things I will always remember,
In the joy of a Cold December.

For You

Friendship is the fuse that lights the spark,
That can give you strength to pull through.
There were times when the road was dark,
But you always knew just what to do,
I never would've come this far,
If it wasn't for you.

My Friends are the best of me,
I know that with certainty,
A crystalline clarity,
Though I don't always show my gratitude.
But please know, this much is true,
I won't use a tired old platitude,
But what I should do,
Is use my last few lines,
As a dedication, just for you.

www.ingramcontent.com/pod-product-compliance
Lightning Source LLC
Chambersburg PA
CBHW062112140826
49812CB00058B/1318
* 9 7 8 9 3 5 7 2 1 3 1 5 8 *